The Flight from Meaning

Other Books by Stephen Haven

Poetry
The Last Sacred Place in North America
Dust and Bread
The Long Silence of the Mohawk Carpet Smokestacks

Memoir
The River Lock: One Boy's Life Along the Mohawk

Collaborative Translations
Trees Grow Lively on Snowy Fields: Poems from Contemporary China
The Enemy in Defensive Positions: Poems from China

As Editor
And What Rough Beast: Poems at the End of the Century
Scarecrow Poetry: The Muse in Post-Middle Age
The Poetry of W.D. Snodgrass: Everything Human

STEPHEN HAVEN

The Flight from Meaning

poems

SL/.NT
BOOKS

THE FLIGHT FROM MEANING
Poems

Copyright © 2025 Stephen Haven. All rights reserved. Except for brief quotations in critical publications or reviews, no part of this book may be reproduced in any manner without prior written permission from the publisher. Write: Permissions, Slant Books, P.O. Box 60295, Seattle, WA 98160.

Slant Books
P.O. Box 60295
Seattle, WA 98160

www.slantbooks.org

Cataloguing-in-Publication data:

Names: Haven, Stephen.

Title: The flight from meaning: poems / Stephen Haven.

Description: Seattle, WA: Slant Books, 2025

Identifiers: ISBN 978-1-63982-185-3 (hardcover) | ISBN 978-1-63982-184-6 (paperback) | ISBN 978-1-63982-186-0 (ebook)

Subjects: LCSH: American poetry--21st century | Poetry—Psychological Aspects | Narrative Poetry | Christianity and literature

For Sarah and Jonah

Nothingness was a wind that changed direction.

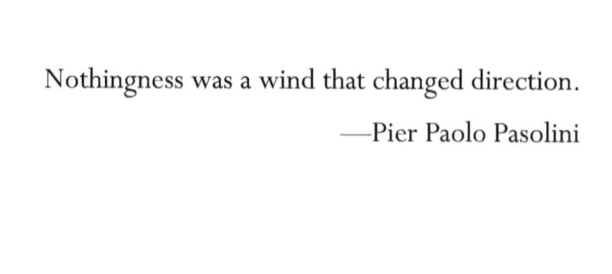

—Pier Paolo Pasolini

CONTENTS

I: WHITE WOLF

Rope Tied to a Song: April 30, 1975 | 3
Solo | 4
*Lines after Pasolini | 6
The Conservative Christian Anarchist | 7
*The Absurd Silence of Nature's Pauses | 9
After Labor | 10
On the Kennebec River | 11
White Wolf | 13
Yanjing Beijing | 14
Housesitting Houston | 16
Chime | 17
Brood | 18
The Gist of It | 19
The Ends of Desire Lost in Plain Sight | 20
Three Short Poems | 23
   Wheelbarrow | 23
   Upstate New York Hymn | 23
   Holiday | 23
Given This Day / *Fin* | 24

II: ON THE VERGE OF WHAT COMES NATURALLY

The Flight from Meaning | 27
The Sacrifice | 29
Equal, Always Equal, to the Inexpressible | 30
Walden | 31
*Orderly Squads of Flowers in the Chaos of Existence | 33
Homage to Sherwood Anderson | 34

Singularity | 36
In an Obscure Scandal of Consciousness | 37
Sugar | 38
Monolith | 39
Black-Eyed Girl | 40
What but Dignity in the Vigil | 42
On the Verge of What Comes Naturally | 43
Iowa City, 1983 | 45

III: DIRTY MONEY
Filthy Lucre | 49

IV: OLD ENGINES
Cambridge, Mass., 1980 | 61
77.15 Kelvin | 63
Salem Easter | 65
Dings | 67
Cracked Springs | 69
Bishop Gilbert | 71
Little Piggy | 72
The Broken Bottle | 74
Rusted Chain | 75
Old Church Photograph | 76
Chagall's *Song of Songs III* | 78
Black Friday | 80
The Furious Patience of the Sea's Blue Grains | 81
Three Stories That House Us | 83

Notes | 87
Acknowledgments | 89

*Poems with a line (or lines) from Pier Paolo Pasolini's poetry are indicated above with an asterisk. In five poems, a single line from Pasolini appears as the title. "Lines After Pasolini" begins with three lines from Pasolini's poetry in the body of the poem. All lines from Pasolini, whether in the title or in the body of these six poems, appear in italics. See Acknowledgments for publisher and translator credits.

I

WHITE WOLF

ROPE TIED TO A SONG: APRIL 30, 1975

The moment the war ends, my father, my mother have gone
To gather their old friends. They have driven to the other side
Of my old town in the Volkswagen. From front porches,
From the rough and tumble of mill yards, American flags
Renounce the colors of love. Somewhere in Saigon
There is singing, there is a monk who does not immolate
Himself in the streets. The killing still goes on.

They will pull the church bell then walk into the silence
Of the chancel. No peace, ever, since 1941.
I am many miles from that place, and yet I feel it
As a kind of home, the thick hemp tied to a song
That lifts me bodily, white surplice over black,
My winged childhood a full foot off the varnished floor,

The basement's trap door. The war goes on.
And yet this moment, the rung cup of other steeples,
No psalm, no sermon, no word for the liturgical hush
Of that shudder, not quite sound, not quite its absence,
In the moment just after. Some blood between them too

But not in this quietude, all their children grown out
From that space. This is the place I choose to lift
A ceremonial glass. The body remembers water, wine,
Music or something like it, the near stillness
Of love as it was and always now will be:
Over the rooftops, each flogged day,
The bell an otter in water, the still black bullet of its clapper.

SOLO

Now it seems your life has been
Nights on late-night dialup, solo in
A communist bloc city.
The television sporting a language
You could never quite fathom
Despite your years of tutelage.
You gather yourself into weekends
With books you've read twice.
So strange to sit at home in Paradise!
But once you sent a cab
To the right Chongqing gate.
Queen Sea Big Shark! Saturday night.
You slipped your key into the wrong

Lock in Dresden, wandered around
Looking for a Wi-Fi connection
Then slept in Niš, rented a four
On the floor jalopy at Constantine
The Great. Then 300 miles south
Where each pristine beach
Was the life you could never keep.
So you ordered another in Macedonia,
Cabbed it in Ubud to the local clinic
Patched your sorry gut gone belly up.
You barely caught the flight, Sita and Rama
On strings, hitching a ride in your one
Zipped bag. (You threw away your clothes

To carry them). In New York Customs
They poked for drugs and parasites.
The wood came clean. Sure enough

You were a gamelan, a puppet man.
But mostly it has been for you
Home seasoning where you tithed
Your yearly dues, did what the locals do,
Soccer, track meets, Sunday school.
Leaned heavily on a mother
Married to a farmer. She taught
Solos to your son, your daughter.
You traveled when your children were grown.
Everywhere you went, you went alone. . . .

LINES AFTER PASOLINI

The birds were singing in the sunbeams
In an intricate uncertain weft
Deafening, vulnerable to existence:

They did not carp of their own demise
Relative to the sweep of land and sky,
How on a peripheral, stubborn perch

No language other than music dwarfed
Their ascent from Mesozoic forests.
The nothing they did not lack

They did not need to own, not one lament
In those hollow bones, swaying in the whorls
Of a single tree like the wind through their

Lost chances. They did not tone
Of the first hard light, first night,
Silence like shards of colored glass

Hanging from a string, metal leavening
A porch beam, or pentatonic
Carved bamboo, clacking where no

Cedar waxwings wobble
In the knit of a tree, almost bundled by these
Burdens of little Being blossoming on Being

Asking of the clouds only a little rain.
Not one had gained so could not lose
A sacramental hue. Everywhere

Around them the one song they knew,
Not one kernel clinging to a cob,
Night nowhere near, night coming on.

THE CONSERVATIVE CHRISTIAN ANARCHIST

To express his contempt for his depraved age, Adams began to refer to himself as a conservative Christian anarchist.
—Ernest Samuels, *Henry Adams: Selected Letters*

Not the kid I once heard on an Iowa City quad
Traveling in a broke-down Dodge,
His girlfriend tapping a tambourine,
Students gathered around the mock of him
Swaying to his rhythm in praise or derision,
Alms in a cardboard box, the pitch

Of that familiar music, that dollar, that dream. . . .
In the wild of that Heartland, the Reformation
On steroids still, our tin-ears tuned
Indian Summer already in bloom. Not the rattle
Of that old croon, but Adams sipping
Like Malbec the new monkey music,

Ideas seasoning for a time, the unfurled world
Spilling always downhill. I told it to Jehovah's
Witnesses who rang my bell. Talk of gypsies,
Nazi Germany, cookies, coffee, both of them
Gracious men. I confess I am
A lapsed Episcopalian: I love my father still.

Come in, come in, let me grind your lens!
Darwin and Adams all but said. It was the eye
That stumped them, light-sensitive membrane
Leaping to perfection, almost inexplicably. . . .
How did we, how might we ever
Begin to see? The sun gathered in places

It had never been, spooned from the single
Celled lotion. At home we begged
The same question, read Rilke, Roethke,
Slurped sustenance from the soup's hot bowl.
Watch your manners! my father said:
"O, Thou Opening, O!"

THE ABSURD SILENCE OF NATURE'S PAUSES

If only you are listening there is somewhere
An old refrigerator straining to beat the heat.

Footsteps from the floor above, the still settling
Of an ancient house. Wind chimes

From your neighbor's yard, beauty and randomness
Wrapped like serpents around a Hippocratic staff.

First nothing, then the furnace kicks in,
An old dryer tosses a pair of shoes

As if they had nowhere in particular to go.
Beyond the distant drum of those hot circles

When my son lay in a Beijing hospital
Bit by a bug, listening through 105 degrees,

No one coined the word for all that ticked in him,
Traveled from a Massachusetts woodland,

The whir of the electric clock, the polyglot
MDs finally scribbling *doxycycline*.

In the hiss of that hospital room, two continents
Held their breaths, until he was his own

Wind instrument, tones, rests drawn from the air
That filled the gap between his teeth. Without measure

And without end, over slow coffee
The traffic slushes by, a plane passes overhead.

AFTER LABOR

Provincetown

Beach-walkers ghost the dry, shucked shore.
A single skiff ices the jetty's craw.
Legacy of the drawn awning,
All prices slashed, the next season flaps.
Terns stitch in a cloud's one tear.
Unmeasured in the wind, always I'll feel
The clef of unchecked mast lines,
Syncopated signatures, slacking in
Autumn's no hint, summer's no longer.
Like a barometer graying in cedar
Only this register: Everything's
Over by a toe. Sheathed in August,
A few feet above water,
A light mistake glides about the harbor.

ON THE KENNEBEC RIVER

The kids are lashing logs together, drilling boards,
Screwing, binding, Sawzalling till they call it
A barge. Freedom's deep in this

Late August Maine when it treads
The river swift, fate swimming fast behind it.
Two canoes, three rafts nothing more

Than old sheathing weathered in the yard
And strapped to a picnic table
Four blue barrels. On top they mount

An awning and a grill, Miller on ice
Side saddling each swamped vessel.
Call it a flotilla, rubber Family Dollar rings,

Everything launched in the tidal flow.
They'll ride to the sea. That's the plan.
Surf the high life back again. They don't fear

The shallows or the Harbor Master's glare.
They laugh off any face-off with the Man:
Boating regulations? Sir, you see

Any boats around here? Five miles upstream
My daughter tells me, *Park your worried
Dad-eyes, Dad! Learn to let it go!* We all take

Shots but mine are photos, cheer
The possibilities of their ripped currents,
No dollars stitched to the river width.

I steer six beers to a rented cabin
Remembering especially a Gallo half gallon,
My father's old Corolla, the black lift

Of an Adirondack highway cutting through
The absence of all color that seemed
Winter's strip tease. Sharp in the face

Of those adolescent midnights
In the tick of that split line
The safe glide home was the lie I told.

Whatever there was of fate and freedom
There was a fishtail between them.
The radials gripped the hard, glazed road.

WHITE WOLF

Beijing, 1990, a seven-year-old laughs at my bulbous nose:
He's never seen a creature quite like me. Great big
Wolf eyes, round, bald head. I bug my eyes out more:

Ghoul! Frankenstein! Chase the boy's mock fear.
Later I catch the chant of street vendors, *Foreign*
Devil! Ghost! Calling to each other as if I couldn't hear.

Then they check out my rank smell: like curdled milk
Someone said, like cheese gone bad. In my wife's translation
I notice something musty, almost sweet: *Sesame oil!* she says,

You are what you eat! Then these years later, to my only son,
Half Boston Anglo, half Han, *At least I knew a year or two*
The weight of carrying my heritage, whole centuries

Of anger alone into a room. "Dad, you haven't got a clue,"
Tourist visit in the stink of this business. My Chinese friends
Pipe in: *At least we stayed at home. . . .* A chant that sours

In Lhasa soars in Beijing! *And you? White scavenging wolves,*
Running in packs, crossing the Arctic gap, howling at the world!

YANJING BEIJING

As if we would remember only this—the perfect dust—
How we slaked it, how it cost next to nothing, twenty-five
Cents American, those sweating green 750 milliliter bottles,
Quaffing that nutty flavor, our privileged deprivation,
Loving it more, that entire year, because there was
In a city of ten million no other lager. This is what
Abstinence did for us. We raised our glasses,

Some of us drank tea. My son remembers still:
Gills golding in the tables, under the glass floor,
The entire restaurant transparent as our mugs,
A breathing viscous world, a huge aquarium,
Grandfathers on either side of him, and one of them
Was missing, no language between them, one of them
Slipping into a broken Russian when his English

Failed him, laughing at the thought that a Slavic word
Might help him, the other grandfather jetlagged,
Ten years older than I am now, carrying always
A fork wrapped in a napkin, saying thank you
In the only way he knew, spearing the dumplings,
100 kinds, pork, carrot, chicken, shredded
Cucumber, cabbage, chives, all due respect

For the distant, honored guest. My son has described
This moment to me, how it appears in his dreams,
His third birthday, when the world was never whole
But seemed to be. No cracks in those tables, no water
Seeping from the floor, no fish thrashing, not even
The cook asking us to finger against the glass
The execution of our succulent dinners. Four years

Older than her brother, even then my daughter ordered
Nothing dead, begged for the life of the tank and cage.
Now I remember no sound but the cries
Of a city that aged me, the slow anarchies of wars
I never knew, mundane fires of families burning still.
The missing grandfather sits at the table, whistling
A Tibetan tune, a Yunnan ditty that always

Gets him killed. My daughter rides the back rack
Of my black Phoenix, my son balances on the bar,
The diesels, motorcycles, flatbed truck-like tricycles
Parting for Moses, admitting us, if only for a moment,
To where we walk on water, raise the glass of the
Unfragmented past, my children, their oldest fathers,
Waving hello, calling from their little eternities still.

HOUSESITTING HOUSTON

When the dog moved out the fleas piled in.
We were right on top of them. Before the jokes
Of how many Yankees the house might turn up, skinned,

We cracked their Lilliputian shells. They croaked
Between our fingers, uncut pincers cured
The lusty leap of a few fat stragglers
Hanging around the kitchen sink, or

We snapped them in a water glass, forever
Certain the tap alone was no solution
Without the human cinch of their pinched backs.

When we moved the touch of their ghostly volition
Jolted in a nightly scratch. We'd ditch the sack,
Flick the switch, scour for the lone stowaway,
Her blood prick in me, bite of each stray city.

CHIME

It lulls me from my back-porch beam
Shimmers like the gamelan I once heard
Wavering in, beyond the edge
Of an Ubud international literary gig,

Lily pads forfeiting center stage,
Vulvas, stamens spread like the fingers
Of an open hand, petals strewn
Along the walks, colored fragments

Of the wind, anonymous, without
Consciousness, shaped by thought,
Carrying an Indonesian tune
Across the ocean in an old gym bag

Till I nailed it to my beam
Where chance makes music
Of its strings, this human place
Pitching at the edge of space.

BROOD

Above the precipice of their own promise
Outside my cabin in Dresden, Maine,

All morning eaglets swung in the crowns,
Squawked at their Moms. Hunger

Unnested them while certain in the lift
Of that watchful moment the mothers' magnificence

Hovered above the shrill, or drilled them out
And were done with it. Nothing already

In their knowing buoyed them the way
A child might thermal into her own currents,

Back walkover on a beam, first roller blades,
Hands free and easy on a red-ribbon birthday,

The strands still flapping from the shiny chrome
But nothing quite that free. One enormous absent eye,

The hollow of that sky, still mothered
In that silence, a loft that never descends

In a black and white muscled sustenance
Ever for them again.

THE GIST OF IT

Maybe it's the body's memory, its muscled bone,
The way a boy plays Rachmaninoff
In and beyond thought, gathers himself

Into a baby grand, the logic of that discipline,
The keynote speakers of that house
Climbing like skilled laborers

The scaffolding around a draped mural,
Wings lifting in an open-air cathedral,
Artisans pausing for bread, for coffee only.

What memory registers
Only in the marrow?
Wood, wire, tusked ivory,

The spontaneity, the control,
In which the body acts
As it was taught to do, and passion rides

That moment like a bull no matador
Could tame, could only kill,
The point of that red grace, that slivered denouement,

Never parting them, always part of them,
The mind inviting this totality in,
The beast in its rebellion, taunting the discipline.

THE ENDS OF DESIRE LOST IN PLAIN SIGHT

Such is the fate of our lone Molly, our trembling podenco,
Who spackles our gray deck white with paint. I will sweep
And patch where she jumps and scratches, a chipmunk's
Warning—*chit, chit, chit*—a few feet from where she strains
The railing with her groomed coat and light-brown mouth.
The rodent's humped life sparks Molly's wire. The two
Crossed ends jump the electric copper. Desire shakes in
The dog. I'm the schoolmarm that tugs her back. Or else
I leash my own sense of self-restraint, observe a mammal's
Nature for a while. At their cross purposes, caught always
In the same burrow, Molly's ADHD triangulates also
The basking hopper, warm on a wound of round
Dirt in our dry grass. Then the surge between the three,
Anything else small and fast, blown leaves and wasps
Molly snaps at, but nothing quite catches her
Quivering tendons like the promise of passion
A few feet above her snout. When I call her back
To her domestic senses, the chipmunk still warns
And scolds, leaving in this equation at least a felt hope
For the fulfillment of dog-wired desire, which has for its
Exact human figure, in this moment, anyway, a boy tracking

His way to New York City, long before the web offered visions
Of naked women to pubescent children. An older brother
Brings the younger to peep before the virginal glass.
The big brother pumps quarters to stage the lit woman
But the boy inside my vision has no hands to deliver
Even solitary pleasure. Or else Tarkovsky's *Solaris*
Where a cosmonaut beds a warm facsimile of his long
Dead wife, her doppelganger some intelligence an alien
Species imposes to relieve or exacerbate his deep angst.

The husband knows the carbon copy will never
Satiate him, and still her perfect breasts are with him
Every interstellar morning. Is she any more inflated—
Canned is the more relevant word—than Molly's carrots
And turkey in gravy—that bloodless meat—
Dished out when the sun sends its fractured light
Daily to the prism of our deck and kitchen? Or we might

Consider the urned man eternally frozen, the "unravish'd
Bride of quietness," who offers nothing in the way
Of a resolving touch. Or Susan, far on the other side
Of Dickinson's hedge, so tall it shadows like a sentry
Emily's widow's walk. "Rearrange a 'Wife's' Affection… Make me
Bearded like a man!" For this our Molly paces the deck, frantic
As Captain Gardiner calling in an endless lick of waves
For his lost and only boy, the ship with Susan Gilbert
For its carved figurehead, the wash of their shared shrub
Another ocean. If only we are listening, everyone
With blood and bone dreams of the woman
Who might call them home, Evergreen the lost
Hovercraft in Eden's storm. Thirteen years after Antony bled
His last goodbye, "Egypt—Thou knew'st" was in actuality
The note that passed between them. All that time
Cleopatra living one door down, *the door ajar*
That oceans are. One afternoon, driving my car, I sang along:

Bo Diddley on NPR. "Who do you love?" Among my children,
I can't speak for any other, and now I count Molly in
That number, love is the easier question to answer, not
So much the paradise Dickinson dreamed of all her life.
Molly squirms at the end of her run. Nearby my wife's
Solar-powered fountain. Depending on the weather
It fires up and peters. Also, there is the feeder
My neighbor built high on a silver pole, his seed stock
Guarded from the ravage of the squirrels. They will
Get there anyway. In my torn rotator cuff, the shell

Of an answer is a road-flattened snapper jerking
Green my morning walk in the direction of its stain.
But who can cinch, spitting, sparking, the frayed south end
Of inflamed desire, tight to its battered Godhead?

THREE SHORT POEMS

Wheelbarrow

This parched pterodactyl
Tucked wings extended backward
Stoops at a drainage ditch
In Ashland, Ohio.

*

Upstate New York Hymn

How could I ever, ever forget
The spring-drunk Chuctanunda
Bleeding, bleeding from the neck,
Its bright dye in that slow gravitas,
The Mohawk's resurrected dark?

*

Holiday

"Now we welcome the New Year
Full of things that have never been. . . ."
That's what Rilke says, the chrysalis
Where we live, everything new
Already old, waking to their new names
And forms, even in the shapes they had before.

GIVEN THIS DAY / *FIN*

Happiness a loaf of bread, the oven not yet cold,
Knowledge the quarter spoon of grain
That leavens dough. All history
That first spread taste, all sustenance that host,
Sips from the tip of the tongue
Then in a final hint of salt, all aspiration comes.

*

When I scissored open her mailed ring
The f-hole of a silent vibrato
Carved a red calligraphy—
Only the word *fin* dangling from a string.

II

ON THE VERGE
OF WHAT COMES NATURALLY

THE FLIGHT FROM MEANING

When the double rainbow shimmered in, we abandoned
The street musician, sat by the ocean-side park
Chewing taffy under those full arcs. . . .

How fully we vanish into them, out on some
Primary edge, the temples of nothing that draw us in,
Light and air, nothing substantially there. . . .

Out over the harbor our still capacity for wonder.

Whatever we murmured in some ambulant pleasure
(Long in that late night the tongue-tipped ladle
Of each breast) which of us now

Will ever remember? Like St. Louis, I thought,
Like some flipped grail, Gothic architecture,
The wharf dwarfed in the lens-snared light.

In the flight from meaning no one fully escapes,
The mass of humanity neither innocent nor guilty. . . .

Then the black and white details of us, fresh cuts
In my old family stone, our wet lithograph,
The unsubstantiated drift of the finite, the infinite,

New love standing before it, late in the summer,
Long in the drive back to where we started.

Even before they vanish they melt into the dark
Room of us, things we long to touch,
Prosecco, bluefish, bread, rosemary sprigs steamed over

The soft anatomy of clams. . . . *And it hardly even rained,*
Someone said, running to the harbor. . . .

No promise, no meaning, not even its brother
Edged in those sun-refracting spans,
The blunt-brushed holes of our homes again.

THE SACRIFICE

Whenever I am day-bruised, night-bruised,
All I have to do is tussle with my angel,
Like Jacob, hip as anyone. Already this morning,
The dislocation, the ache in my bone,
Angling for a foot of turf, digging in
For that new territory—*Oh Israel! Oh Canaan!*—
Along that hoary line of scrimmage.

Before I crush him without hurting
A halo of his head, my chest against his chest,
The power of those wings blurring
The room we're somehow floating above
Till it holds also you, my love,
The sheer communal bungle of our bodies,
Death itself still talking, my scarred life

Bushwacked at the slipped, trenched root,
As in Catullus's wedding songs
The town in a paean for Hymen,
The groom already swollen,
The bride welling to take that loaded limit,
The chorus chanting *OK, so now they'll have*
To stop shopping it around. Still the desire

To stuff Ipsithilla, persona non grata
In that crowd, come off together
Straight nine times, laughing, crying,
And feathered in your hair, moving forever
And nowhere near, love's hardtack,
That clutched pivot, the angel, you, me,
One tight scrum in that trinity.

EQUAL, ALWAYS EQUAL, TO THE INEXPRESSIBLE

That's what the stoic said believing the pond of his own head
Flush as any flush thing, lake or sea, winter's runoff
In the drink of eternity, the rock, the pulse of utter solitude
In which the only conversation is your own, single splash
Of a rose outside a leaded window, its inexpressible attitudes,
The train strumming by, the four-year-old drilling the floor
Above your head till you know you'll soon be dead,
The trees' thin crowns, not yet winter in their stammer.

You wish to take yourself inside the bamboo wind chime
Breathing of Indonesia, rising among born-again cicadas
Seventeen years under, a litany of home
Clacking in wooden bones. The lost art of repose,
The flapped, worn-out blind of clicked, webbed time,
Serial surrogates displacing the places you'd been
The touch of them nothing till you web them up again,
The mind's muscle slackening in the saved chipped page.

Out of darkness the ear will lead us. You must be very quiet
To hear blind Milton chanting to his daughter in the space
Our century vacates. So the window of a single rose.
You sit there remembering your father reading
Sunday afternoons, a glass of sherry floating in snow,
Heifetz in Beethoven's concerto, this wooden wind,
These insects slumbering through
Long gestations of some mind, conjured in quietude.

WALDEN

Whatever Walden is to me—we swam there two Julys—
I hope to skirt that never-ending trope,
Drowning like a pilgrim in that pond.
We pushed past mothers and their kids,
Cedared summers in Wellfleet cottages,
Past foreign languages that hummed across
The narrow circle of that one dirt path

Tossing stones from their home countries
On a mound that almost sanctified
An eclipse of the Old Manse.
One Japanese devotee, his beard
A gnarled shrub in sandy soil
All the way from the hagiography
Of Tokuyama City, bruised by
The crowd, the boom boxes, the concrete

Latrines on his holy shore, pushed past
The diapered, dapper beach
And in a mud-stuck tortoise's
Mammoth shell found a native genius
Wallowing in some self-made myth
We saw beneath the wooden footbridge.
That was Nobuhiko, my old friend,
That was thirty years ago, and now I am

Alone the swimmer in dead center
Who treads the ninety feet beneath,
The sun clarified by a few lingering clouds
That filter him, buoy him above
The silt-free water. A quarter mile out,
Floating on his back, ears under, going

Nowhere fast, he finds the mind
Slung in a parenthesis of sky, as if his head

Were helmeted by the entire stratosphere
That leaves him nowhere, leaves him fast
Pulling toward the one canvas bag
That holds his shades and mask,
Glad for the ring, the click that offers him
The promise of a door, two dinner plates,
Two lit candles, one old dying dog.

ORDERLY SQUADS OF FLOWERS IN THE CHAOS OF EXISTENCE

Each limousine the pinwheel of a funeral.
Fifty percent cuts in the U.S. nuclear arsenal.
The night nurse easing your thin bottom

Cold to your last commode. Or the telescope
That once outdated Hubble. Each prayer.
Each tank of air. The work we do. Once above

North Africa each Black Hawk helicopter, the pilots
In their bubbles. The way the British
Love to queue. Dust grazing the gown

Of the Confucian scholar, fat in the Maoist mode.
Your last dollars gone to origami
In the glass jar of the casino.

HOMAGE TO SHERWOOD ANDERSON

Each year a new mall fountains up, the Food Court assimilates
Its corporate heart into the lost pasture of the village square.
Swine once scavenged there, and men, flapping in leather helmets,

Hurled hard bodies at one another. Further back they swung
Fat sticks at rocks. The milk once loved udderly froths at Starbuck's.
A soccer mom spoons five dollars' worth of guilt from a daily cup,

Her covenant with the mantra and hue of the lost American Dream
Of the Beautiful. How can she find it now when they couldn't then?
The world past, the one passing, meld into the mile she has already

Hoofed this morning. They've named a shoe for her. Not quite
Ovid's ideal, not quite Emerson's. Mall Walkers they call them.
If only you are listening, you can hear her mutter, *Too often, George,*

You stay too much indoors, though that is not exactly what she says.
*Hello, I am Billy Pilgrim. I am her husband. This is my translation.
I have been to Chicago and back again. I am originally from New York,*

*Call it Ilium. Where I must go again. I simmer in the tent of my own head
In this oasis, under* The Cleveland Plain Dealer's *spread. While I steam
My wife fattens. Retired by trade, I fix the vision of anyone who does*

*Not dream in the spit and polish of a Tralfamadorian Porn Queen.
Come in! Come in! Let me grind your lens! It is really my mother
I am talking about. It is Dresden. I would really rather speak*

*Of something else. I am Willard. I am Bailey, some kind of George.
Or the Rev. Curtis Hartman. It has taken me this lifetime
To find the divine manifesting itself in the barren shelves*

Of the last two shopping days left before Christmas.

When my wife wanders I rush through the aisles
Sharing my vision, these silk accoutrements, the sheer possibility

Of Kate Swift's body, the wildest dream of my wife's family's
Underwear industry. Who would ever imagine
The wonder of such interiors, bamboo flourishing in winter,

Ohio offering through its maternal crack
The fecundity of its dark soil, trunk of a living palm
Thrust in the break of the Food Court's tile. In Dresden

At least a few people crawled out of the steaming buildings
Despite our best intentions to stew them: *Hello I am Odysseus*
Come to throw out my own grandchildren. The Northwest Passage

Cuts this way again, suspension cables, the railroad spanning
Manhattan, Brooklyn, striking the tuning fork
In which we hear the O of the Orient, that dollar, that dream.

You who have congregated always by the sea, lift up your sushi,
Your curry, your whole bread. I ask you to consider the luxury
Of the American interior, how even now it pearls in our sleep,

Victoria's Secrets not quite beyond the Half Moon,
The Hopewell's reach. Banked by your great river,
In Tompkins, Battery Park, stay with me awhile, hear me out.

SINGULARITY

That's what we are, each of us
A dead star, constellations
Where we have gone

Missing through the slips
The swallows of those holes
In the measure of our time

We call it singularity
Our collapsed commons
Seeding the newborn's

Soon forgotten furl
A sweetness slipped
Into the box of a primary grade

Light spun like cotton candy
Where we tucked our pencils
Our erasers, September then after

The Ferris fields a gaping O
The grasses beaten down
And overgrown. . . .

A nothingness—that substance—
Descant that can hardly sing
Past noon, bruised in that womb

Snares in a smothered start
Light years it has taken us
Seeing from that dark

IN AN OBSCURE SCANDAL OF CONSCIOUSNESS

> The discovery of the amplituhedron could cause an even more profound shift.
> That is, giving up space and time as fundamental constituents of nature.
> —Nima Arkani-Hamed, Professor of Physics

Each human place jungled in the dark, our pup tents
Staked to infinite night. A machete is a light.
Torches the British call them. We say flashlights.
Mime shadows the vaults of our long rooms.
In the living place, where we lay down our Hearts,
Track the Queen of Spades, the trick is to bring
The Jack of Diamonds home. Now I see more clearly

Our loomed images: Even the airbrushed canvasses
Of where we live strain the guy ropes of endless night.
Each eye alights on mosquitoes sizzling in the flare,
Each silhouette fires from our fingertips. We gather
Like mammals in domesticated puffs of air, the cold
Herding our bodies onto each other, cleaving in a way
Illuminates us, beyond any ken. Then a new lens,

This little amplituhedron, our geometric gem, magnifying
The agoraphobia of where we live, the minuscule
Infinities, fire in the hole, a burning ember,
A curlicue. Against space and time we release
Our smoked signatures, our little peep holes,
This light rebel, jewel through which we find the Joan
Of our staked minds burning in a radix of sky.

SUGAR

I have heard the Japanese burst bubbles
To pollinate their flowers, but I prefer
The hummingbird sharing its nectar
With a bee or two, those light hovercrafts
Stitching the air with their slight wings
But only one of them a needle nose,
1000 beats in the very minute its muscle
Drills the white stamen around which grows
The deeper purple labia minor
Of the violet hibiscus, all of which offers
All the way through October
A taste of its delicate petals. Today we sip
Our coffee, having given up our lumps
Of sugar long ago, but there is a sweetness
On the tongue not only from the cream
We still indulge as we overlook
Our neighbor's shrub, two town criers,
Two back porch birds, the feeder
Of our table, our folding chairs,
Our caws diminished for a moment
But rising like prisms you can see
On the thin soapy film, the small round
Wands we blew our breath through,
A breeze that stings ninety degrees
Across the ocean and the Boston burbs,
Saying in the dart, the tender and the blur
This is the violet, all is well with the world.

MONOLITH

Still the poets wrote of their mothers, their fathers,
Of their favorite rust-red houses in the deepest recesses
Of loved cul-de-sacs. They scraped skateboards off ramps.
In their gray hour they plumbed the funeral pyre
Of blossoms they discovered endlessly exorcising
And reinventing themselves, the plumb or level line,
A vantage point, a holocaust of mind
Casting colors like a film projector, how such things
Never gained a foothold in nature, so why ever
In poetry and architecture, new figures, new orders
Coined for each new day, each one fully temporary,
Absolute and necessary, of nature and man-made,
While in the pup tent of the central cortex
In the form of Kubrick's black monolith
There was no chatter and this time no laughter.
Though something shattered nothing broke.
From their old chairs the poets took note,
From the language of love and dust looked up
And cupped their spent fathers, the lovely interior
Made by their mothers, and the curve of each year's flowers.

BLACK-EYED GIRL

Upside-down she ventures to the last leaf
Out on a branch so thin we hardly think
It can hold her weight, fur nearly woven
Into those light tendrils. That silver lookout,
Her entire body, swings with the wind's
Noncommittal hymn. I think she is carrying
The heft of the entire evening as she cups
The breeze with her flattened belly.
She seems to hang there to no purpose,
Upside down for the sheer joy of it. We fear

She'll tumble twenty feet, then she turns tail,
Flips to a higher, stronger tether, upside
Down again, seems to eye and listen as three
Neighbors sing to the delight of everyone
Stationed on pandemic porches, Van Morrison's
"Brown-Eyed Girl," beyond the point I can see.
Then the thin promise comes through clearly,
To stage a concert from the open door of the lead's
One-car garage, each mic'd Friday. Hope is the entire

Neighborhood hooting from the distance of our
Windows and yards, calling to the musicians,
Calling though they admit they never learned
"Stairway to Heaven," "Cowgirl in the Sand."
They sing for nothing, sing for the lost
Cause of their ambition, bars that will
No longer pay them, bars they offer anyway

So that even our one daily splintered spirit
Hangs in a pure abandon beyond the manna
Of samara, acorns, the one pistachio we dropped

From last night's deck empty of guests. Hangs
Beyond any thought of what we imagine
Brings her to float spider-like as she sends
A curious thread out of herself, watching,
Listening, coursing through a blowsy evening
Where free from the last shred of a metal strap,
All the way through The Crickets's light tattoo,
Beneath the paused gray of her daily acrobatics,
One loose downspout rattles a back-porch post.

WHAT BUT DIGNITY IN THE VIGIL

The night nurse quibbling with the old GP,
The becalmed family lobbied in everything.
But they can't agree. More or less morphine?

Then the coroner calks the door
Their cargo embargoed, down to the last apple,
Scurvy in the hold. Realtors, creditors, conjugate

The numbers of their deep harbors: Always room
To pay some more, foam from the ocean floor.
In this you're meant to swing, hit perfectly

The back walkover on the beam, high five
Your work colleagues, walk the dog six a.m.
As always, flag of your old repose,
That slit sail, that white rose.

ON THE VERGE OF WHAT COMES NATURALLY

The moment Menelaus stalks
Paris to nip the edge of war
Helen's in a fit: She's a Spartan

After all! This is her swan song.
She sticks with her old flame,
Prayers in Menelaus's name!

Nine years a long time never
Tucked in her mother's arms.
Heaven offers only this fallacy,

One husband's death or the other's.
There is for constancy only
The father of the soon sacked city:

Priam catches Helen's grief
In the hard streets, calls her dear,
Absolves her of everything

The gods stir. Even then
She wishes Paris's black blood
Bubbling around the shaft

Menelaus is soon to toss.
But where is the radiance
In that? Aphrodite seems to ask.

Only air at the point of M's
Flung spear, the gathered men
Muttering of fate and heaven,

Lust or luck in the vanishing.
Then beauty's sweet talker,
Favorite son and flatterer,

Floating on a pallet of light,
A verb he conjugates
Above his marriage bed.

When Helen finally takes him,
The lovelier, weaker man,
The oracles of their bodies,

Those concentric circles,
Drift from forest to wilderness,
The gods peering behind

The curtains, the tongued O
Of that hymn, stranger
Than dissonance, unison.

IOWA CITY, 1983

I remember best the Oxford shoes, the three-piece suits,
How he always sat in the back row of our summer class,
Striped tie, maroon and gold, if I recall that one day right.
He was ten years older than the rest of us who Heartlanded
Whitman, Dickinson that July. Iowa City, 1983, no A.C.,
Landlocked in that humidity, except in groceries,
Theaters, maybe the rare café, a hamburger
And milkshake town in those days, ninety degrees forcing us
Out to Dingleberry's Quarry, where we swam
Without our skivvies, cows wandering into the opposite
Mucky end. We dodged their pies, occasional
Water moccasins, perched on rocks, dove in the deep spots.
But it was coffee after class when Craig joined our jeans
And T's. When he packed a pipe and lit it, we broached
The subject: "What's with the suit? I mean, really?"
"The distillation of evil from the claims of innocence is ironic,"
Reinhold Niebuhr said. "I'm broke," said Craig, a victim
Of circumstance. He was rich, once, so the story went.
Now he had nothing but old fancy suits his parents
Once bought him. I didn't like to doubt
Another man's story, didn't know him, glad to share
A cup of coffee, talk about my pending trip.
My girlfriend and I would eat nothing but oysters
And bluefish. But what about the apartment, he asked?
He needed two weeks to get back on his feet.
I don't remember the entire circumstance
That led to *yes*, or the exact chain of events that never
Consulted my lover, but he moved in the day we left,
Ours a two-bedroom second story, nothing fancy.
One window was broken when we came back.

Glass shards littered the nook we squeezed
Into our galley kitchen. Yes, he slept in our double bed
Just as he said he wouldn't. "What'd you expect?"
My girlfriend asked. The bourbon gone, a couple
Hairs still glued to the empty bottle, our double Dutch
Porcelain stuccoed all over, egg yolk, spaghetti hardened
In its dead sauce, dried mint chocolate chip, the package
Gracing the garbage. Two weeks' worth of God knows what.
I reached him by phone in our favorite watering hole
Where each night T.A.s held prisms to the human
Stars again, glinted also against a sign that flashed
The clarity of the Rockies and everything we drank,
Artists, writers, a couple historians, one crazed evening
A theologian, all of us ganging on my lovely girlfriend
Who refused the earth would go to the tern
Of an intercontinental missile, and then the flock
Would follow. . . . In so many words
God so loved the world. . . . Whenever she left
To pee or fill her glass, we laughed in a wisdom
Beyond our drafts, jeered about unschooled
Peasants, plebians. Craig asked did I find
The check he left? "Must have blown out
The blown-out window. . . ." "Stay right there," I said,
"We can talk it over a glass." "Tell you what,"
He said, "Lend me your car, I'll drive to Davenport,
Pick up everything to make amends." Two weeks later
He hit me again: AT&T billed for long-distance,
Numbers that offered nothing when I called them.
Then finally his grandmother: "Happened like this
Many times before. We've washed our hands of him."
My girlfriend left me shortly after. I wondered
What it meant to be a good partner, or if Niebuhr
Was too hard on his fellow citizens, spent one long
Lonely night with my girlfriend's ex-bosom friend.
I remember best the cartography of each failed kindness,
At four her Irish daily milk and tea, smooth as Wild Turkey.

III

DIRTY MONEY

FILTHY LUCRE

I'm not what I ought to be, I'm not what I'm going to be,
But Lord, I thank you, I'm not what I was.
 —The Rev. Gilbert Haven Caldwell, Civil Rights Activist

The poems of the ax murderer burn in the sun,
Speak of love. In the twist of this
Lit calligraphy, among the other kin,
We might consider him Gu Cheng.

*

John Hope Franklin, the American historian,
Questioned the quarters the tour guide
Never unearthed for him when he took
In the sights at Monticello.

*

We post our slavery on our bills,
A currency we carry daily in our folds.
How else might we pray for a Bauhaus
Coffee table, however faux,
Chagall's *Song of Songs* framed above
An Italian sofa my wife once truly loved?

*

Or anything else we might throw
Our G. Washingtons for as we count
The score: B. Franklin only six,
G.W. 300, Jackson topping
A centuplicate, even Ulysses S.

With a single man servant, our defunct
Two-dollar icing the cake,
600 not counting his sons, his daughters.

*

The poems of the ax murdered in the son
Swirl like flotsam, like ash, liturgies
That wax, sealed in the mother's blood.

*

Only Lincoln's fin the sad exception
But he was always divided, depression
Clipping the heart of his economy
Mondays and Saturdays, Sundays too,
And every other day of the week
As well. *Mea culpa*, Alexander Hamilton.

*

No, we didn't exactly chat about it
At the Warrensville Heights Y.
After a good sweat, 100 daily stomach
Crunches, among the other stuff,
We'd catch a bite, a draft at the local pub,
Sam, Al, me, the light end of a long day.

*

"Sam," I said, "I know why we keep
Pumping the light stuff. We think
We're running out on death?" *As long
As you ain't chasing it!* Sam cracked back.
We laughed, all of us pushing seventy.

*

We covered the bases in my three years
Lifting there, the cost of Viagra,
A bill your old lady should gladly pay
One young dude grunted out
Like he was gifting his babe
The fundamental joy, 350,
One bent bar, bouncing off his chest.

*

Not even the Three Kingdoms will speak
Of the poet self-slaughtered in the sun,
His wife's German lover missing her
By hours when her crushed husband
Caved her skull. *Don't take a walk there,*
Sparing only their young son. *Don't take*
A walk, sealed in the mother's blood
The taut tropes of a father's love.

*

Deer edged close to the city, far side
Of the lot. We could see them out
The Y's back windows. It was there Sam
First called himself "The Mayor":
Be a new face around here, you get the tour:
Cardio, strengthening, the sauna, the pool.

*

Somewhere around November, Al said
He might actually enjoy his T'day dinner
If only your kind hadn't killed all Brotherhood
Around that table. Not one of those slaves
Was carrying a Bible when they come off
The ships, not a one.

*

Yes, I didn't exactly say, but let's not short
The friendship between Bradford
And Massasoit. It took a second generation
For Plymouth's children to jettison
The few surviving kids and women
Into the Caribbean. "Small scale genocide,"
I confessed. *No scale about it*, Al said.

*

"Only love interests me," Chagall once said.
"I am only in contact with things
That revolve around it. . . . From the head
Almost nothing, from the heart?"
How else might the fish of a quarter
Moon hook a jeweled bird's beak
Gaping to gobble it? Mixed all the way
Through the lover's blue, a kiss
Recalling Klimt, a wreath, a wake of flowers
Stirring the palette of the Torah's child.

*

Hey Pretzel Man, where you from, anyway?
Stretching forty minutes each morning
Just to earn a good walking day.
"Snow, North Country, somewhere
Near Albany. . . ." *Can't be as cold as here*,
Wind off the lake forty below
Windchill in a Bomb Cycle.

*

Sam's oldest dropped the kids with him
24-7. The son will never earn a pension
From the local UAW. Sam worked
The Nautilus to help him carry
The kids who call him Poppy.
Then we inevitably came around
To Lebron, the one, the only,
The favorite son. Maybe Russell,
Maybe MJ, Chamberlain
The greatest one, *Lebron, Lebron, Lebron.*

*

Still in the good graces
Of the retired auto and steel workers
Of Warrensville Heights, Ohio,
Later that year Kyrie Irving rolled
The fast lane back to Boston.

*

We have done those things we ought
Not to have done, we have left undone
Those things we ought to have done
And there is no health in us.

*

Al couldn't imagine too many
Black people in my New York valley.
I always considered my family
Free soil only. Then my sister
Sent me everything Ancestry.com.
My great-great grandmother,
A Carolina Belle, up my mother's line.

*

Belle Cohen's grandfather, a rabbi,
Traded in everything that made
Good money. We always suspected
My mother's love of her mythic
Southern gentility. Then in the digital
Head count of an 1830 Census
The "Schedule of Whole Persons
Within the Division allotted to. . . ."
What I never knew, Al and Sam,
When we drank a beer or two. . . .
In thin pencil, our ancestors' names,
Jacob's Canaan leading the way,
294 slaves.

*

We thought the scales might split the legend
If we glared hard at the map, Solomon
And Jacob Cohen contra dancing
With my father's family—E.O.
And Gilbert H., our Methodist abolitionists,
Both of them bishops: *No one can throw stones. . . .*
Not even the Quakers . . . are without blemish. . . .
No land for the chiefs of the rebellion,
Homesteads for the loyal bondsmen.

*

The Rev. Gilbert Haven Caldwell,
Civil Rights activist, and his father,
Tapped the name of our "white
Antebellum MLK," carried it,
Preached it dead into the dark
Of two more centuries.

*

Winters on Division Street
The African Methodist Episcopal
Crossed my father's Anglican:
No look passes off the dribble,
Alley-oops to the man in the middle.

*

At six foot one, I planted my pivot
In the paint, Taylor, Teabout,
His diminutive brother Mike,
The old Armory gym, worn leather
Softening a shooter's touch,
Everything steaming through
That winter-drummed dried oil.
Squeak of that old wood floor
The moment you opened the door.
Luke Beekman's son snagged
A Chicago million, cleats dug into
The Bears' line of scrimmage.

*

The end is in the beginning and lies far ahead....
Heft them together the best you can,
This prism, *these fragments shored*
Against my ruin.... Ellison banging
The pipes of Waldo's prison
From which the Old Possum
Dangles a key: "You kinda young,
Daddy-o...." "I yam what I am,"
Said God, said Invisible Man,
Said Olive Oyl's sailor man.

*

Luke Beekman's ancient of days
Great-Grandmother Grace
Ironed for my mother. Mrs. Blood,
We called her. She watched us
When we were toddlers.
*My mom and your mom got to jabbin
And they are jabbin still,*
Henry Blood, ninety-five years old,
WWII vet, told me on the phone
The day the Menands Cemetery,
Outside Albany, sifted my mother
Through my father.

*

Alan Miller, my old college friend,
Sold 9,000 copies of *At the Club*
Hanging in Oakland's gay pubs.
Forty years later, we talked for hours.

*

Whatever I was, whatever
I'd become, by our own hands
They were axed, we were masked,
They were murdered in the sun.

*

Al called me *white boy*, meant it kindly,
Asked me over for egg foo young,
A Cavs game on his flat screen TV.
Every house sported the same
One-car garage. Row after row
Tight brick two-stories. He cracked
The front door screen, watching for me.

*

As late as 1900 Grace Blood
Was an indentured servant.
My mother wrote a book about her
That oral history one small part
Of the jagged story.

*

Al built a goose egg on each arm
Three years after spinal fusion.
Biceps and triceps and jointed titanium.
First time I hung out there
I wondered what kind of trouble
I slipped down his basement stairs.
We lit a bowl, toasted a Bombay
Sapphire gin.

*

Hidden in the tryst of a thousand poems,
Laved in the mother's blood,
The barking unicorn of the orphaned son.

*

Sam tucked two pistols beneath his bed.
For my own safety he'd never take me
Home to meet his babies.

*

Hey Pretzel Man, Sam said, *bet you never met
A Black guy as hip as Al on that subject.*
Al summed it up best: *Guess what, Steve,
You're up next!* He gifted me

His father's medallion, Baker's Union
511, and a little brass pipe
I keep hidden in my grandfather's desk,
The gift that keeps on giving.

*

Then three years later I'm East again:
They rip the largest bone, power saw it
From my body: Outside the PT, waiting
For my pain no gain, my cell rings.
Al hands it over to Sam: *Now don't be
Taking none of those opioids. We're coming
To Boston. See if we do. If we don't be finding you
Back here soon, we're sleeping in your living room.*

IV

OLD ENGINES

CAMBRIDGE, MASS., 1980

> Where can we live but days?
> —Philip Larkin

I thought of the strange things people say, a boy crying
Calendar, Calendar Day! as if we woke to moments
That had no place on the page, so loud I remember
This late decade, the kid lugging till then
Unheralded *Heralds*, or were they *Globes*
The length of the train, calling to everyone,

Now especially to me, the doors gumming shut
Like a toothless mouth, trading his smudged stack
For change, his fingers blotter-stained,
The weekly arts section tucked inside
The articles of war, leavening the front page,
Mugabe riding Nkomo in those days,

The lights blinking off then blinding us again,
The kid urging us to act quick, as if we risked
The pivot of our planet, *Woden's Day*, *Thunor's*,
Venus budding profanely in *Vendredi*, *Tiw's Day*
God of law and war. . . . I spread the insert
Across my knees, Spider John Koerner crooning

At the Plough and Stars, the Blacksmith House
Waxing Piercy's female moon, Bly on a dulcimer,
His tone-deaf God-awful voice broken to the day
No *I am* made. Then the ripped umbilical cord,
The saturnine drift of Kubrick's lost astronauts,
The train rocking us back, a star for each lulled hour,

The contra dance of each clipped day
That spins so fast you will fall without the fixed
Eye of a partner nailing your glance.
This boy, this town crier, calling from a place
Cracks time, cracks space. If you listen,
This is his offer. . . . He is only asking for a quarter.

77.15 KELVIN

After her second shot the artist starts to talk about
Cryonics of all things, the initiate of her boyfriend
Who attends such conferences. . . . *Freeze me, baby!*

He once said to her, at the height of their bodily passion.
Of all the absurd, most passionate, climactic words
Surely there are worse! One can only imagine

What jettisons between them. 12,000 bucks
For the brain floating in vitro, free of the scuttled
Skiff of the line-tangled body, a cool quarter mil

For the whole nine yards, every finger, toe,
As if at 77.15 kelvin we found heaven,
The boiling point of liquid nitrogen

Flushed through the xylem of each dead organ
The bodies upright in their silver cells, one new
Hal singing "Mary had a Little Lamb," each eyebrow

White as snow. One by one the banks drain
The trust accounts. Ward of the frozen state
Your life-long partner croons by the power

Of his attorney. No prince wakes you
Ever from your glass sleep, or duly waits on you,
Vigilant as a Millerite counting on some

Nineteenth century New York hillside
The clouded arrhythmia of Christ.
The artist pours another straight up, no ice,

Figures the crystalline rapture's a vessel
Rigged with time, scaffolds into nothingness,
Ghosted with minds.

SALEM EASTER

The inkwell of that royal purple
Smeared Easter on our fingertips:
Our lunch was an egg dyed
Onion-skin red on a seat cracked
For John Burroughs. Above us,
Five airy blue Eastern Orthodox bulbs
Trumped the plain cut truths
Of the old slate stones, our hands cold
Against those skulls, their crossed bones.
Then the mercy of dried flowers
In little gold piles, then the rows
Of less grave centuries, where masons
Winged the marbled dead to cherubs'
Lighter epiphanies. The trick
Of each reappearing dove
Fluttered in the wave of a silk red scarf.
In just a time of little matter
There were angels everywhere, lattes
Heavenly along the Wiccan shops,
Palm readings fifty bucks a pop,

The mall right down the road,
One kid on the Witch Walk
Riffing for his dinner in a topper
Calling to the crowd, *Maybe we can
Even see them now.* In cameo
A teenage shade blurred through
The clips of our chipped phones. . . .
Then beer, chowder, the softening harbor. . . .
We logged into Hawthorne's light,
Glad he was born there, the old Bay State

Tuned sharply to its minor key
Far from that other clef, the wicks
All Concord burned where he was buried.
We dreamed of a seaside condo, the train
To Boston, slapped sails tethered
To our late mornings. Seasoned
In that choir, singed in one hymn
With all the old-time barkers
We knew that in America
The deeper spirit is the darker.

DINGS

Now my car has many colored dings
More in a single year than all the time
I lived in Cleveland. White smeared

Over my fender, black dot
In the middle, red swaths along
The running boards, me and my Sonata

Spinning one bent song, slipping
In lots of privilege
Where they save my favorite spots

Flipping the bird at rush hour
Forgiving the little love tap
Of the parallel park, bumping fenders

To find out just exactly where we are,
Each scratch, each imperfection
The city in blossom, flowering right

Outside my home. I rub my hand
Against them, throw out
My GPS, renounce the lane intrusion

Warning system, the automatic park,
Knowing my job to find myself
Is finally to get lost. These days I ride

Through the city remembering old ways
Thoroughfares without street signs
Of my twenty-second year, opening through a maze

Of Boston's little neighborhoods,
Driving Memorial, Soldiers Field Road,
Thinking I've come home. . . .

CRACKED SPRINGS

What do I see tailgating behind me? A '74 Chevy Nova hatchback,
Two doors, the rust and gold so close I can find in the rear-view mirror
The steel plate I riveted above one rotten wheel well. Wherever I've been
Pulls up fast behind me again, those six cylinders never leaving me
Broken on the highway, driving Houston, Iowa, New York City,
My first ride firing its star power even in Beijing. Even there
I felt it tailing me with its two back broken springs, the headlights failing
In the snow on a drive from Peterborough to Somerville,
    the night ticking off
The windshield so I pulled close to a semi and rode those running lights

All the freeway home. That year in Beijing my Nova was a black
Phoenix three-speed: I followed the lead of fire, ash, wheeled wings
All around me. Under their hats my kids' heads bobbed
Like egg yolks leaning to custard in the caps of their half shells.
We shot each intersection's gap like an open field running back,
My daughter, six years old, sidesaddle on the back rack, on the bar
My son, bouncing on the level, my arm around him. I wondered,
Even then, of the kid I met teaching at the MANCI Ohio State prison.
In all languages the blacktop, the traffic signaled No Stop, All Go,

The gray spill of arterials into one massed circle. He was serving
Twenty years. Then the stillness of the dead in its freeze-frame time,
Soused with silence. It landed him finally in a room where we held forth
On fate and freedom, the thin white line broken between them,
The boy, the men, living it beyond any class discussion,
This one lit instructor wondering how to love all the different voices,
Dreiser's Hurstwood, just past forty, never exactly choosing
The stolen money. Beyond any reason, lured from the windy city,
The brief delight of his nineteen year-old Carrie. She leaves him, finally,

To the Hudson, the Bowery. In the night it comes, in daylight too,
One moment we were never meant to choose. I asked the class
What they made of that. One student coughed at a friend, a pair
Of busted glasses swollen around his head. *Yeah, just like you
Never meant to shoot that guy!* Then the room broke to laughter,
The boy grew quieter, twenty years younger than those men.
Outside the room, across the maw of the open yard,
In their solitude the guards questioned the necessity
Of any text I carried. They wouldn't bankrupt their children,
The prisoners attending free, to gas on about some dumb-assed yarn.

BISHOP GILBERT

Now the rich claim squatter's rights in Cambridge.
In the storied quad each year my colleagues
Visit the distinction, *Who shall be considered human?*

America always botches the question,
My unschooled upstate New York friends
Never even wishing to take part in the discussion,

Banned from the committee
On Respect, Integrity, the hallowed halls
Neglecting, anyway, to invite them to the party.

Who shall live on thy Holy Hill?
I queried my ancestor Bishop Gilbert H.
He owned a nineteenth-century three-decker in Malden,

Shared handsomely in the flourish
Of a New England economy
That built the slavers' boats, textile mills

Weaving cheap cotton from Southern plantations,
Hartford insurance commanding a clean fortune
In human trafficking. He harbored in his churches

No distinction between black and white
So presided over white flight, till in late years
He traveled to see the Mother Country

Died of some disease contracted there
Leaving me to beg the question
Who would he have his daughters marry?

LITTLE PIGGY

First autumn after college, Charlestown High,
1979: Teacher aides hawked the halls
Like bouncers in a bar, like Nick Buoniconti
Dishing collisions to anyone near them.
The busses, police cars, steamed outside,
And in my classroom one girl, Rose,
Built like a linebacker herself,
Calling me John Boy, my cheekbones,
My white skin, *Goodnight, John Boy!*
She followed me from class to class
Threatening my ass, flirting, flicking
Her lighter beneath the window shades,
Daring me to call her a name.
Or Darryl Williams, fifteen years old,
Shot from a rooftop, three Irish kids
Catching him with a twenty-two beneath
The helmet of his halftime huddle
So that he never moved the first-down-
And-ten chains again, never carried
The pigskin. In the cafeteria high

Chinese kids steered clear of the front lines,
Savored what their mothers taught them
Of the succulence of their brown sauces,
Not one white, no black tight around
Their four-toned tables. Or the angel dusted
Irish kid, hanging the full length of his arms
Outside a third floor window, just for the sheer
Wilding of it, his hands swollen at the sill,
His friends tugging each red finger, saying,
This little piggy went to market, this little piggy

Had none, laughing hysterically, finally
Gathering him back to the room
Where they promised to wait for me
After school: *You think you're going home?*
In the yardless yards, patches of grass,
Little scattered oxygen masks. Everywhere
Around me, they never showed. Bus doors
Opened like salvage or salvation, safe
Passage past the monument at Bunker Hill.

THE BROKEN BOTTLE

What was that mistaken midnight, when without
Your brother, drunk with the swish of your
Own promise, you wandered to The Broken Bottle?
High School basketball shooting star!
Which of the parched men cheered you
Earlier that evening, then ushered in the mug
Of each gaunt letter, each lost job, then held
You down in the quick of that moment,
Signed for no reason you could ever imagine
Their names on the bloom of your cheeks?
The initials of two slashes on each?
The shattered glass secured you to the mirror
Of your unshaven future. Each morning now,
At daybreak, they glare from your sleep-drenched face.

RUSTED CHAIN

Sometimes the mind rises only into its own sky
The day gone to wind and last night's rain

Our names skipping like flat rocks
Across someone else's hopscotch

Where once you scratched your Xs and Os.
Or was that tic-tac-toe, tally where no one

Should ever win, though you can blunder
Badly, losing in the lens

The spot that marks your name
Your old bicycle with the rusted chain

Leaning against the willow of your boyhood window.
Over dinner, mumbling to yourself, when you come out

Of the rain, what will you say?
A box of chalk dissolving on the sidewalk,

A dead dog trailing you
Running to your whistle?

You have gathered there in this way station
Of momentary prayer, before the broken bread.

Well, it's only your mother's sauce,
Only a taste of her leavening the pot.

See, it must happen this way: Around
The set table, this new silence, this radical.

OLD CHURCH PHOTOGRAPH

Your father's gray tower, his old hard drive,
Sparks to life, every kid coat and tied
Except one rebel in a sweater, open shirt
Beneath his cocked smirk, everyone else
Sporting black cloth but you and your brother,
Youngest ditties in the circa '64
Men and Boys Choir. Easter gleams
In your light jackets. Only you two beam,
Wink through the doom. Behind you

Gothic stone, the ivied rectory you once
Called home, your father back row central,
A head taller than the other men. All the names
You almost know, the one kid in glasses,
Dead the day before his only marriage,
All of you on the breeze of a bus ride down
To New York City! The World's Fair!
Progressland! six rotating stages, carousel
Of how our digs have changed, iceboxes,

Street lights, the range of our robotic lives,
Sparking new the old routines of death and love—
"A fellow named Tom Edison." Twenty-four-minute
Revolutions. There is no seventh stage
And on it you finally see the digital green
Of a taxi ferrying you an hour early
To the terminal. A satellite tugs
You toward your final love. She asks
A haunt to snap this "great and beautiful

Tomorrow, shining at the end of every day,
Just a dream away. . . ." Past the gate

The stewardess locks the door.
The pilot offers nothing about the weather,
Destination, point of departure.
Almost inaudibly, as you click into your seat,
Through your absent earbud the cough,
The hum of an old engine, their muted *nay,*
Nee, ni, no nu, the old valved voices warming up.

CHAGALL'S *SONG OF SONGS III*

The inverted splash of a yellow church
With a turquoise bell tower drives
The color the earth shares with the sky,
A purple reign not even Prince imagined
When he threw his Mad Cat Anderson
Up in the air in a tribute for George Harrison.
Some riff that gently weeps and will not end
As it bubbles also in the bridal pansies
Carried in one hand. Circles like the orbs
You used to dip and blow, the slippery suds
Bursting over the pipe's one plastic bulb,
A purple concentricity sung in unison

By everyone, unheard by anyone because
This is, after all, only a village gathering
In a brushed Talmudic oil. They field around
Their favorite fauvist lick, gather in the silence
The sun a tambourine refracted in diamonds
On the floor of a pool where you spent
A summer's heat one afternoon. The bride's veil
Cups the ecclesiastic torch of her red hair,
A winged candelabra rises above the cornucopia
Of a jaundiced moon, upside down and fallen
In the lake below. Even now you hear their vows
Curve in a dark blue groom along her shore.

Upright in their ceremony, they reappear
Doubled in white at the edge of the canvas,
Spooning each other in the moment just after.
Maybe only in this altered cleaving
A peace that passes its own sense and season.

The town sends its accompaniment
Through a woodwind to a painter's fingertips.
He tilts his easel, teaching his few students.
Below them, the wrong way up, where love
Burdens sorrow, in water, or on it,
An old man's cane probes the hidden place
Where an artist threw his instrument, high above
The king's staged son. When it never fell back down,

Seemed to disappear, no one ever shared
The sleight of hand that simply vanished
Above the crowd when the backstage crew
Reached for that strummed flung sound.
(It hung in the scaffolding like a kid
Flipped on the high bar of a jungle gym,
Veiled utterly by the open curtain's fringe).
The stunned stars milled around as the last
Note dropped. When Prince slipped off
Leaving a reverberating hole in the air
Even Chagall's crowned mythic beast, llama-like,
Craned its head to look again.

BLACK FRIDAY

I lit the doomed colony
Of a candelabra on the altar
The black cassock of all history

The stupendous monotony of mystery
Singing on its knees
In minor thirds only

Even the hooded cross
A falcon in the dark
Through it all the light dripped in

Bent taper, brass lip,
Lick of one flame
Wick to wick

THE FURIOUS PATIENCE OF THE SEA'S BLUE GRAINS

Great whites stoked the sparse, strafed shore:
In some new way we never saw one
Except on the surfed web, or on our friends'

Clips flipped open in galleries, celled dorsal fins
Beyond the breakers' break. We stared down
Swells so small you could hardly call them

Open water. Seemed the Sound.
Somewhere in a pure upsurge of feeling
In an instant the sealed world relieved itself

Of one less bark. No love like theirs,
An atavistic passion nuzzled to a gill.
Then the blur of their gestation, alpha pups

Wolfing weaker womb mates. Sun screened
We webbed it up, their intrauterine communion
Like bloody blended Marys on the rocks:

Framed in the tidal wash a clipped man staggering,
Punching back. We barely stuck a toe
Into their ace in that hole. Right down the road

Each leaf shining in water so still
Light that never registered on the pond lens
Was our own repose. The litany of a breeze

Stoked the surface of a breath. The unswayable sea
Surged in a peck of sand. Poised above
Our sandwiches, our towel spread, framed

In each stalked season, each airbrushed harbor,
Only the osprey—bird of prey—
Bobbing, barely moving, on the marshes.

THREE STORIES THAT HOUSE US

My father thought the Anglican liturgy pure poetry, once,
300 people chanting in the multi-colors of the chancel,
Saying on cue *We do!* Though they might have answered
Otherwise in their own living rooms, together
They committed to many things, the dignity
Of every human being, the baby lifted high above
My father's head, as in a ceremonial sense
Of his long-limbed, six foot three, a little thin
But with good bones, white-cassocked, black-haired
Public self, splash of a maroon stole. He muscled
That small life up and down the aisles
As if he shouldered some new luck each one of us
Should psalm, finally laying the child in the arms
Of an old woman. Too weak to join the family
At the altar, she let out a brief cry. Just so
We might plant a tree that will never grow
Before we die. Just so my father,
Old Navy officer, gathered his charges to sing
Though there were people they favored killing
Other side of the world, and some owned factories
The others had to work in, material cutters,
Machinists in the toy shops, the wages
Dust those men, those women took a match to
Late afternoons, Luba's Tavern half a mile downhill
From the three-thirty buzzer, $3.12 an hour when I worked there

One college summer, sliding a circular saw just shy
Of my fingers, or turning the same screw
All dead-day long, the communion wafers of salt tablets
By the coolers, the floor fans idle for fear
Of what might fly and perch for an August lifetime

Under the eye, the drip of each minute a kid
Bored and hanging over your shoulder
In a plugged-in instant ready to stir up trouble.
We'd sleep for ten minutes at ten and two,
For a full half hour at noon, sprawled on stacked
Pallets we woke to the yawn of table saws
That kicked back clouds of snuff, the cut
Particle board rolling off the other end almost
Faster than we could catch and stack them,
Forklifts spinning 360s, 180s, leaving in their wake
The hot blast of the exhausted past, the breadth
Of our own day, that did not winnow through
Green-painted windows we pulled open with chains.
Air hockey, foosball games! They made thousands,
Never brought one home. Still, they played them
All night long, like a coy girl they hunted,
Haunted, never quite made, folding on the bar
A wad of cash in the trust of her glass's watermark,
Teasing her hair in the bathroom lull of the pub
For a drink or two, playing them all the way through
The Cabbage Patch Doll boom, the cars in three shifts
Parked up and down the road, my father's pledges
The children of skilled weavers who skipped England
After World Wars I & II, and some were troubled kids
Who sat with their mothers in the back pews,
Spun the rock to me Fridays and Saturdays,
The dead spots in the armory gym stealing the ball
Like an invisible point guard leaving you
Only air in the gap of your lost dribble.
Once I was ashamed, I was afraid to speak in public

My father's public name, how he might never say a word,
Sitting with the farmer who with the family car
Backed over his own child and thought he hit the dog,
Saying nothing out of the ordinary, nothing more
Than that man's name, over and over as the drive's

Gravel flew again, the neighbors bringing alms
From their kitchens, as if the body must be fed
In the wake of the dead, or saying less, as if silence
Had its own dignity, its own music, and it wasn't poetry,
Though it circled impossibly its own meaning
The way language does, the way a thing can never quite
Be its name, not in such a moment anyway.
And maybe that's for God to say, if one can ever stake
A claim for the narrow of *that* inadequate name,
The way the word sweetness, say, the idea of it,
Never quite lolls honey on the tongue,
Never dribbles it out of the corners of your mouth,
Your love's sweet spot mixing in your beard
Till with the back of your hand you wipe
That syrup, lick your fingers, and in the aftertaste
Poetry is there, if luck is with you, if your heart is full.
Or else I defer to the woman whose son lay in the bruise

Of a New York State prison, or was himself that bruise,
Where my father drove her all those years, since she had no car,
No other way to offer the tight vigil of the guards
Her pockets emptied of her son's penance, of anything
She might have carried, shoeless for a moment
Before she passed the double-steel reinforced doors,
Crossed the courtyard, the snipers hidden
In their towers. What would she say? Who was the priest
Who came to her never bearing God's name,
Offering rather something simple, a ride down the highway,
Waiting in the silence of a Tiparillo,
A '67 Mustang that never purred, black as the clothes he wore,
Never geared to any practical thing, spark plugs,
Clean oil? Each night my father downed
A couple dry martinis, invited any neighbor to join him,
Never the woman he drove down the highway.
She was drunk the last morning he went to her door,
Every piece of him somebody's funeral,

Formal, regal, almost military in his bearing,
The full stature of his light frame leaning against her railing
Until she swore she would never go back there again
With him or anyone, *So what are you always bothering me for?*

We are always only becoming, we can never quite *be*,
Each of us failing the office of our own names,
The three stories that house us, the given, the familial,
The one in between, as if there were something
The years can't figure, each of us clouded
In the uncut crystal of our own nomenclature,
The cuckolded husband who never cried foul,
The seed glowing in the womb of the child,
Some new realm jeweling above the gossamer
Of the burgeoning woman's unbroken hymen,
Strange as the stories of our own scratched soil,
The earth itself sharing a tale of where
We've been, where we are going, an accident
We can never quite track, much less name,
My old neighborhood, my Italian friends,
What I once called them, drifting behind me
Like a mantra, word that has no meaning,
Door that opens nowhere for anyone
But for me always, rocking the way
When he was gone my father did one night
In the needlepoint of his mother's favorite chair
And if he spoke I can't remember anything
But the enormity of that calling,
God and his absence, against any utterance,
Not of the blood, the body only,
Melting on the tongue-tip the untold story.

NOTES

The epigraph for *The Flight from Meaning* is quoted from Pier Paolo Pasolini's poem "Presence," translated by Stephen Sartarelli, *The Selected Poetry of Pier Paolo Pasolini* (University of Chicago Press, 2014).

"The Flight from Meaning" and "The Sacrifice" are for Alessia Marshall Mays, with thanks for our shared years.

"Filthy Lucre" is for Alan Davis and Sam Wright, also for Alan Miller, with thanks for our friendships. Thanks also to the Warrensville Heights, Ohio, YMCA, for a warm welcome during my Cleveland years.

The Rev. Gilbert Haven Caldwell quote that appears as an epigraph at the beginning of "Filthy Lucre" is from a United Methodist Communications video; transcripts from the video appear online at:

https://www.umc.org/en/content/gilbert-caldwell-voice-for-justice-and-human-rights

"Filthy Lucre" quotes briefly from Eliot's "The Waste Land." The source for the Chagall quote in this poem can be found at https://woodshedartauctions.com/understanding-the-stories-of-marc-chagall/

The Bishop Gilbert Haven quote in "Filthy Lucre" can be found in William Gravely, *Gilbert Haven, Methodist Abolitionist: A Study in Race, Religion, and Reform, 1850-1880* (Abingdon Press, 1973).

Three brief quotes from Ralph Ellison's *Invisible Man* (Second Vintage International Edition, March 1995) appear in "Filthy Lucre."

The poem "Singularity" is informed by the article "We Are Dead Stars" by NASA astronomer Michelle Thaller. The article appeared in *The Atlantic Monthly,* May 13, 2014.

In "Iowa City, 1983," the Niebuhr quote is from *The Irony of American History*, "The Ironic Element in the American Situation" (University of Chicago Press, 1952).

The epigraph for "The Conservative Christian Anarchist" appears in Ernst Samuels, *Henry Adams: Selected Letters* (Harvard University Press, 1992).

The quote from Rilke in "Three Short Poems," 'Holiday,' is from "Letter to Clara Rilke, January 1, 1907."

The epigraph at the beginning of "*In an Obscure Scandal of Consciousness*," by Nima Arkani-Hamed, is quoted from Natalie Wolchover's article, "A Jewel at the Heart of Quantum Physics" (*Quanta Magazine*, September 17, 2013).

"Cambridge, Mass., 1980" is for Rosa Lane, sister in poetry, sister in life.

"Old Church Photograph" quotes from the song "The Carousel of Progress" by Richard M. Sherman and Robert Sherman.

"Salem Easter" and "Chagall's *Song of Songs III*" were written with love for my wife, Gordana Mihajlovic.

"Salem Easter" is informed by *In Small Things Forgotten: An Archaeology of Early American Life,* by James Deetz (Knopf, 1977).

ACKNOWLEDGMENTS

Thanks to the editors of the following publications where some of the poems in this book appeared:

The American Journal of Poetry, A Poetry Congeries (Connotation Press), *Arts & Letters, Asheville Poetry Review, Blackbird, Chautauqua, The Common, Communion Arts, European Journal of International Law, Image, Interim, The Literati Review, Live Encounters, The Montreal Review, North American Review, Saint Katherine Review, Vox Populi.*

"Rope Tied to a Song" was a finalist in the 2018 Public Poetry Power competition and appears in *Power: A Public Poetry Anthology*: http://www.publicpoetry.net/2018-winners/.

"The Ends of Desire Lost in Plain Sight" was a finalist for *Asheville Poetry Review*'s William Matthews Prize for best single poem.

In earlier, shorter form, *The Flight from Meaning* was a finalist for England's International Beverly Prize for Literature.

Excerpts from *Poems* by Pier Paolo Pasolini, translated by Norman MacAfee. Translation copyright © 1982 by Norman MacAfee. Reprinted by permission of Farrar, Straus and Giroux. All Rights Reserved.

Quotations from *The Poems of Emily Dickinson*, edited by Thomas H. Johnson, Cambridge, Mass.: The Belknap Press of Harvard University Press, Copyright © 1951, 1955 by the President and Fellows of Harvard College. Copyright © renewed 1979, 1983 by the President and Fellows of Harvard College. Copyright © 1914, 1918, 1919, 1924, 1929, 1930, 1932, 1935, 1937, 1942, by Martha Dickinson Bianchi. Copyright © 1952, 1957, 1958, 1963, 1965, by Mary L. Hampson. Used by permission. All rights reserved.

Thanks to the Provincetown Fine Arts Work Center, the Ohio Arts Council, and to the Djerassi Foundation for grants and residencies that supported the writing of these poems.

Many thanks also to Greg Wolfe, writer, editor, Slant Books publisher, and long-time activist in the arts in so many, necessary ways; to Rosa Lane and Julia Thacker for their reading of many of these poems in earlier form; and to my poetry colleagues and friends from the Ashland MFA Program, Kathryn Winograd, Ruth L. Schwartz, Angie Estes, Alex Lemon, and Mark Irwin, for the good spirit of ten great years.

This book was set in Perpetua, designed by the British sculptor, artist, and typographer, Eric Gill, in response to a commission in 1925 from Stanley Morrison, an influential historian of typography and adviser to the Monotype foundry. The design for Perpetua grew out of Gill's experience as a stonecarver and the name pays tribute to the early Christian martyr, Vibia Perpetua.

This book was designed by Shannon Carter, Ian Creeger, and Gregory Wolfe. It was published in hardcover, paperback, and electronic formats by Slant Books, Seattle, Washington.

Cover art: *The Community of Those Who Have Nothing in Common* by Mark Blavat. 54" by 58", oil on canvas. Used by permission of the artist.